Este pasap
This passj

CW00376741

PASSPORT

This passport provides the holder with the facilities for normal transit in accordance with international treaties and conventions.

Este pasaporte brinda al titular las facilidades para su normal tránsito de conformidad con los tratados y convenios internacionales

Autoridad / Authority

PHOTO/FOTO	TYPE/TIPO P	PASSPORT / PASAPORTE **0123456789**
	NAME/NOMBRE	
	SURNAMES/APELLIDOS	
	DATE OF BIRTH/FECHA DE NACIMIENTO	
	DATE OF ISSUE/FECHA DE EXPEDICION	

<<<<<<<<<<<< TRAVEL <<<<< VIAJE <<<<< 1234567 >>>>>>>>>>>>
<<<02022020>>>>><<<<<IMAGINOMIFUTURO>>>>><<<<<>>>>><<>>>>